Diving to a Deep-Sea Volcano

By Kenneth Mallory

Houghton Mifflin Company — Boston 2006

www.houghtonmifflinbooks.com

The text of this book is set in Apollo.
The display type is set in Aquinas.

Library of Congress Cataloging-in-Publication Data

Mallory, Kenneth.
Diving to a deep-sea volcano / by Kenneth Mallory.
p. cm.
Includes bibliographical references.
ISBN-13: 978-0-618-33205-2
ISBN-10: 0-618-33205-7
1. Submarine volcanoes—Juvenile literature. 2. Hydrothermal vents—Juvenile literature. 3. Hydrothermal
vent animals—Juvenile literature. 4. Hydrothermal vent ecology—Juvenile literature. I. Title.
QE521.3.M26 2006
551.2'3—dc22
2005025449

Printed in Singapore
TWP 10 9 8 7 6 5 4 3 2 1

Photo Credits

Page i: The Stephen Low Company; ii: The Stephen Low Company;
iv: Emory Kristof, National Geographic Society; 1: Rich Lutz and
Woods Hole Oceanographic Institution; 2: Rich Lutz and Woods Hole
Oceanographic Institution; 3: J. M. Edmond, courtesy Woods Hole
Oceanographic Institution; 4: Woods Hole Oceanographic Institution;
6 (map): Jerry Malone, based on work done by Robert Vrijenhoek; 8
(art): E. Paul Oberlander, Woods Hole Oceanographic Institution; 9:
The Stephen Low Company; 10 (map): Jerry Malone; 11: Rich Lutz
and Woods Hole Oceanographic Institution; 12: *top*, Emory Kristof,
National Geographic Society; *bottom*, Robert Ballard, Woods Hole
Oceanographic Institution; 13: The Galápagos Rift 2002 Expedition,
funded by NOAA's Ocean Exploration Program, the National Science
Foundation, and Woods Hole Oceanographic Institution. Photographs
courtesy *Dive and Discover;* 14: Al Giddings and Woods Hole
Oceanographic Institution; 15: Anthony Tarantino and Woods Hole
Oceanographic Institution; 16: *top*, Rich Lutz and Woods Hole
Oceanographic Institution; *bottom*, Rich Lutz and Woods Hole
Oceanographic Institution; 17: Woods Hole Oceanographic
Institution; 18: The Stephen Low Company; 19: Hanumant Singh and
Woods Hole Oceanographic Institution; 20 (map): Jerry Malone; 21
(art): E. Paul Oberlander, Woods Hole Oceanographic Institution; 22:
Kenneth Mallory; 23: The Stephen Low Company; 24: Al Giddings
and Woods Hole Oceanographic Institution; 25: Woods Hole
Oceanographic Institution; 26: Rich Lutz and Woods Hole
Oceanographic Institution; 27: Woods Hole Oceanographic
Institution; 28: Woods Hole Oceanographic Institution; 29: Woods
Hole Oceanographic Institution; 30: Margaret Sulanowska, Woods
Hole Oceanographic Institution; 31: *left* (art), E. Paul Oberlander,
Woods Hole Oceanographic Institution; *right*, Kenneth Mallory; 32:
Woods Hole Oceanographic Institution; 33: Rich Lutz and Woods
Hole Oceanographic Institution; 34: *top*, Emory Kristof, National
Geographic Society; *bottom*, Woods Hole Oceanographic Institution;
35: The Stephen Low Company; 36: Emory Kristof, National
Geographic Society; 37: Woods Hole Oceanographic Institution and
Mike deGruy; 38: *top*, Fred Grassle and Woods Hole Oceanographic
Institution; *bottom*, Al Giddings and Woods Hole Oceanographic
Institution; 39: The Stephen Low Company; 40: Rich Lutz and Woods
Hole Oceanographic Institution; 41: Emory Kristof, National
Geographic Society; 43: Rich Lutz, Tim Shank, and Woods Hole
Oceanographic Institution; 44: *top*, The Stephen Low Company; *bot-
tom*, Rich Lutz, The Stephen Low Company, and Woods Hole
Oceanographic Institution; 45: Kenneth Mallory; 46: Kenneth
Mallory; 47: Emory Kristof, National Geographic Society; 48: The
Stephen Low Company; 49: Anthony Tarantino and Woods Hole
Oceanographic Institution; 50: *top* (art), E. Paul Oberlander, Woods
Hole Oceanographic Institution; *bottom* (art), Jet Propulsion
Laboratory; 51: The Stephen Low Company; 52: The Stephen Low
Company; 56: Kenneth Mallory; 58: The Stephen Low Company

Contents

After its dive, the deep-sea submersible *Alvin* is hoisted back aboard the research vessel where it undergoes maintenance in its storage hangar.

First Dive to the Abyss

R ich Lutz peered out a tiny porthole just bigger than the size of his fist. A mile and a half below the surface of the Pacific Ocean, it was pitch black. The only signs of life were scattered white specks of tiny deep-sea water creatures called plankton dancing like tiny fireflies.

Suddenly he heard the whirring of the submarine's thrusters, propeller-driven engines that enabled the sub to maneuver at the bottom of the ocean. Then the lights came on. Beams from spotlights at the nose of the submarine illuminated a field of sediment and rock that seemed as desolate as the surface of the moon.

"What's that?" Rich asked his companion, Dr. Howard Sanders. A round white object the size of a volleyball sat on the ocean floor just beyond Rich's porthole. "It's a protozoan" was the improbable reply. Rich's jaw dropped.

Protozoans are single-celled animals usually seen only through a microscope. What an exciting and strange new world Rich had just entered!

A solitary rattail fish surveys a desolate, sediment-covered ocean bottom. Before the discovery of hydrothermal vents, most people thought this was what every part of the deep sea looked like.

Rich Lutz (*foreground, right*) looks on with his mentor, Howard Sanders (*middle*), as they prepare for Rich's first dive to a hydrothermal vent in 1979. They were about to plunge to one of the greatest mysteries on earth.

When Rich went on that dive in December 1979, it was his first time in a deep-sea submarine. Although he may not have shown it on the outside, the little boy in him was just bubbling with excitement. He remembers feeling like "the new kid on the block with all the gods of deep-sea research as shipmates."

Rich could not have picked a better submarine than *Alvin,* the Woods Hole Oceanographic Institution's research submersible. Neither could he have found a better guide than Howard Sanders. As an ecologist, Dr. Sanders studied communities of deep-sea animals and how they fit together. He would help give Rich—whose special area of marine biology was the study of mollusks such as clams and mussels in the shallow sea—the big picture of life in the deep ocean.

"It was *Alvin* dive number 986," Rich recalls. "As we began to travel along the bottom, I remember worrying that we weren't going to find the mussel beds that we were looking for. Then, suddenly, as we came over the crest of pillow lava, the community spread out before us. I remember thinking, *This has to be the most exciting environment I've ever witnessed!* It was a truly magical dive."

The tubes of these red-tipped worms called *Riftia pachyptila,* first observed and photographed here at a Galápagos Rift vent in 1977, were much larger than the other worms familiar to most scientists. Worms found on a coral reef are often only a few inches long—these stood fourteen to eighteen inches high. A pink "vent" fish called a bythitid patrols the area. The squiggly lines on the rocks are serpulid worms. Other circular white dots are mollusks called limpets. This oasis of life was completely unexpected.

Deep-sea spaghetti worms drape the volcanic rock like strands of pearls in regions just outside of hydrothermal vents. Normally these kinds of worms dig into the sea bottom's mud for protection, but they seem to survive here despite being exposed to potential predators.

The excitement Rich felt that day went far beyond a trip in a submarine. Imagine the thrill of taking part in one of the great new discoveries of twentieth-century ocean science—it was almost like finding life on Mars, or the beginnings of life on Earth.

Two years earlier in this same spot—250 miles northeast of the Galápagos Islands off the Pacific coast of South America—a geologist and a chemist discovered an oasis of life that took them completely by surprise. They found giant crimson-tipped tube-worms six feet long, ghostly white crabs and "squat" lobsters, shimmering fish called eelpouts, fields of orange animals shaped like dandelion flowers, giant mussels and clams, and animals that inspire names such as spaghetti worms and rattails. In the utter darkness of the deep sea, there was an unforeseen community of animals, a strange new frontier waiting to be explored.

Understanding the Deep Sea

When Rich was growing up, very little was known about the deep sea. Most people considered it an underwater wasteland of mud and worms. As scientists developed new technologies to explore the deep, they revealed a clearer picture of what the planet looked like thousands of feet below the ocean's surface.

The first scientific attempt to map the world's oceans was the Challenger Expedition, organized by the British in the late 1800s. The scientists hung weights on the end of miles of hemp rope and piano wire to measure depth. In 1919, French scientists obtained the first recordings from an acoustic echo sounder, ushering in a new era of sonar (SOund NAvigation and Ranging). Sonar electronics emit sound signals and then turn the echoes into visual images, which scientists use to map the ocean floor.

Using sonar, scientists proved that the greatest mountain ranges on earth were not on land; they were in the deep sea. More than 40,000 miles of undersea mountains called the mid-ocean ridge (a chain of connected volcanic mountain ranges) encircle the globe from the Arctic through the Atlantic, Indian, and Pacific oceans. How did these mountains get there?

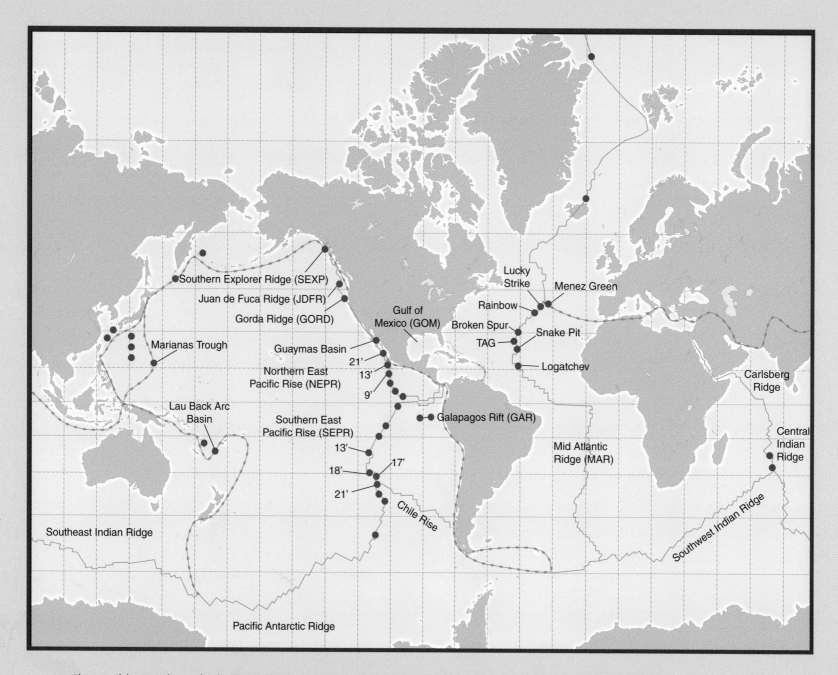

Southern Explorer Ridge (SEXP)

Juan de Fuca Ridge (JDFR)

Gorda Ridge (GORD)

Marianas Trough

Guaymas Basin

Northern East
Pacific Rise (NEPR)

21'

13'

9'

Lau Back Arc
Basin

Southern East
Pacific Rise (SEPR)

13'

18'   17'

21'

Chile Rise

Southeast Indian Ridge

Pacific Antarctic Ridge

Gulf of
Mexico (GOM)

Lucky
Strike

Menez Green

Rainbow

Broken Spur

TAG   Snake Pit

Logatchev

Galapagos Rift (GAR)

Mid Atlantic
Ridge (MAR)

Carlsberg
Ridge

Central
Indian
Ridge

Southwest Indian Ridge

This world map shows hydrothermal vents discovered to date, including the Nine North site indicated by the number nine off
the coast of Central America in the Pacific Ocean. Dots without names are among the most recently discovered. Scientists are
discovering new vents all the time.

In 1973 a joint science mission between the United States and France called FAMOUS (French-American Mid-Ocean Undersea Study) set out to explore the Mid-Atlantic Ridge that runs down the middle of the Atlantic Ocean between Europe and Africa and North and South America. To see these mountains for themselves, the scientists sent *Alvin* and a French companion sub, *Cyana*, to a world they had barely imagined.

At the top of the ridge they found a giant trough a mile or more deep and three to six miles wide that ran the length of the mountain range. Scientists call it a rift valley. Hot molten magma—a fiery porridge of minerals and metals just below the earth's crust—rises here in volcanic eruptions, constantly creating new ocean floor. Like squeezing a ball of clay and letting it ooze through your fingers, molten lava thrusts out of openings in the rift valley, spreading new ocean floor like a giant paving machine.

DEEP-SEA HOT SPRINGS

How can a deep-ocean community of animals thrive on hydrothermal vent fluids poisonous to most other forms of life? We know that photosynthesis is the basis of most life on earth. On land and in sunlit waters, plants use a green chemical called chlorophyll to capture the energy of light and convert it to the energy of food—which for plants means using water and carbon dioxide to create sugars and starches.

Plants pass their food energy to plant eaters such as rabbits on land and algae-eating parrotfish in a coral reef. These rabbits and parrotfish in turn become the source of food and energy for meat eaters such as wolves and barracuda. But how could the same foundation for life work in the deep sea, a world of utter darkness with water pressure so powerful it could crush an armored tank?

In the world of hydrothermal vents, single-celled microscopic organisms called bacteria play the role of plants. Bacteria are everywhere—on land, in fresh water, and also in the sea. Like plants, bacteria produce their own food, so they don't need to eat anything else. Without the light plants depend on, some kinds of bacteria get their power to manufacture food from a chemical compound called hydrogen sulfide.

Hydrogen sulfide is a molecule that is toxic to most living systems. It's the same chemical compound that makes a swamp or a salt marsh smell like rotten eggs. Just as plants "eat" light for their energy, bacteria eat hydrogen sulfide. Huge mats of bacteria feed animals farther up a food chain that range from worms to deep-ocean octopuses. Scientists call this kind of energy conversion in the deep sea "chemosynthesis" because bacteria get their energy to make sugars from chemicals.

Hydrothermal vents are the engines for life thousands of feet deep. When water seeps down through cracks in the ocean floor, it is heated by the giant furnace of molten rock called magma that is at the center of the earth. When this heated water emerges through openings called hydrothermal vents, it carries compounds such as hydrogen sulfide and metals such as copper and zinc that it gathered miles beneath the sea floor.

CHEMOSYNTHETIC FOOD CHAIN

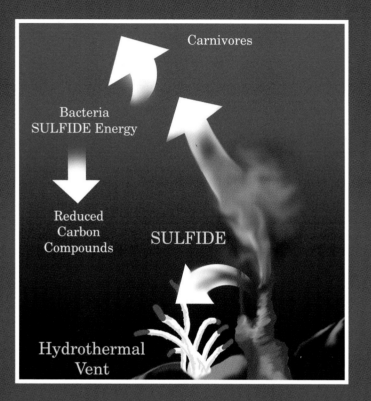

PHOTOSYNTHETIC FOOD CHAIN

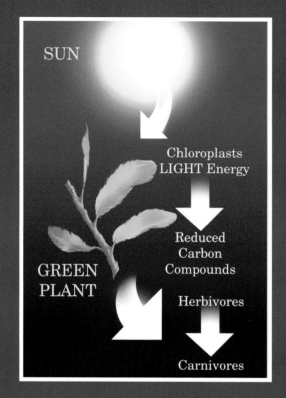

1. Hydrothermal fluid coming out of vents contains hydrogen sulfide.
2. Microbes living around the vents take up hydrogen sulfide, oxygen, and carbon dioxide from the water.
3. The microbes get energy by breaking down the hydrogen sulfide. They use this energy and oxygen to convert carbon dioxide into sugars.
4. The microbes release sulfur and water.

1. Plant leaves capture energy from sunlight.
2. Leaves take up carbon dioxide from the air.
3. Leaves use water and the sun's energy to convert carbon dioxide into sugars.
4. Leaves release oxygen into the air.

All living things need energy. Animals and people get their energy from the food they eat. The plants on land and the microbes that live around hydrothermal vents, however, need to make their own food.

Oceans occupy more than 70 percent of the earth's surface and contain 328 million cubic miles of water. Scientists have mapped less than 10 percent of the mid-ocean ridge, which produces about 95 percent of the volcanic activity on earth. Every year it also creates an amount of new oceanic crust that would fill up the Grand Canyon in nine years.

The rift valley that *Alvin* and *Cyana* scientists witnessed supported a theory that geologists had been arguing about since the early part of the twentieth century, called plate tectonics (tectonics is from the Greek word for "carpenter" or "construction"). The earth is composed of a thin crust that encases a thicker mantle and a fiery hot core. The crust is a collection of twelve huge slabs of rock called tectonic plates. They are sometimes hundreds of miles thick, and they fit together like puzzle pieces on the surface of the earth. Some plates are continental (form continents) and others are oceanic (forming sea floor). They all float on a vast sea of molten rock that forms the outer layer of the earth's core.

Plates constantly shift in a process called continental drift. Sometimes they pull apart, sometimes they collide to build mountains, and sometimes they slide under one another, disappearing into giant deep-sea trenches. The Mid-Atlantic Ridge is just one of the many boundary lines, called "spreading centers," where two plates are spreading apart—in the case of the Atlantic, only about an inch a year.

Black smokers are spectacular hydrothermal vents. They can be dangerous for submarines because they spew hot liquid well over three times the boiling point for water on land.

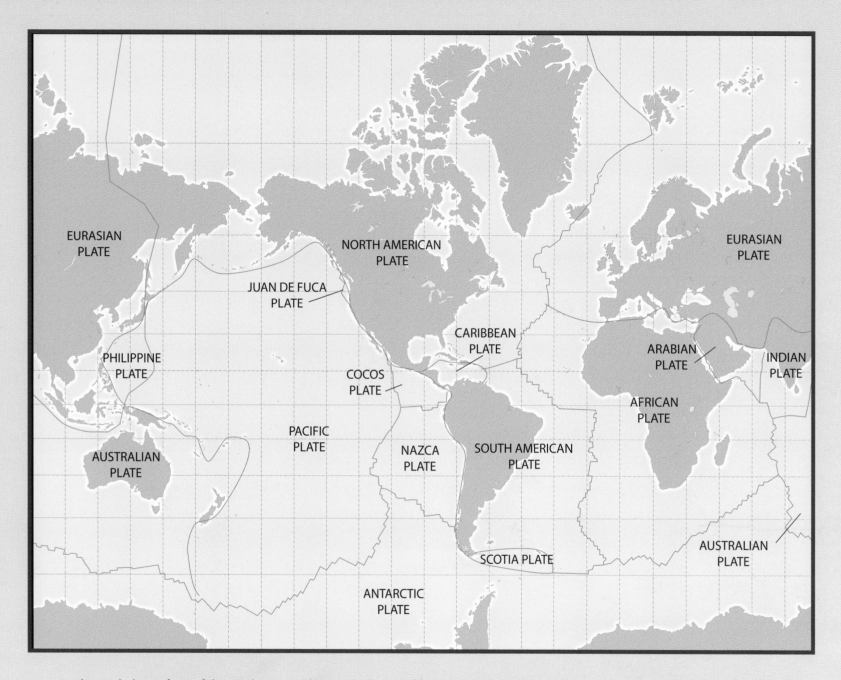

Underneath the surface of the earth is a rigid outer shell about fifty miles thick (100 kilometers), which is divided into ten major and numerous minor plates. The plates may move apart, collide, slip under one another, or move edge to edge at the boundaries that divide them. Separation of two plates along a common boundary is producing the volcanic activity at Nine North.

Discovering Life Where Life Doesn't Belong

Rich Lutz and Howard Sanders were looking for a bed of mussels near a hydrothermal vent, which would help them begin answering some basic questions. How old were the vent animals and how fast were they growing? Previous work by one of Rich's colleagues seemed to suggest that a typical deep-sea clam that measures a third of an inch across was a hundred years old. Did all the animals of the deep ocean grow so slowly?

Rich's early work studying clams in the shallow waters of Chesapeake Bay had prepared him well for science in the deep sea. As a student scientist studying mollusks—a group of invertebrates including clams, mussels, limpets, oysters, snails, sea slugs, octopods, and squid—he had devised experiments that tested how temperature affected the growth of clams. Like the rings of a tree trunk, clams have annual growth rings on their shells. By measuring the distance between each clam ring, Rich discovered that higher temperatures made clams produce more shell than usual.

The growth rings of clams like this one from shallow waters in New England help scientists measure their age.

Top: Giant clam (*top*) and mussel (*bottom*) from hydrothermal vents. One species of hydrothermal vent clam (*Calyptogena magnifica*) grew three hundred times as fast as a typical deep-sea clam that had grown a third of an inch in a hundred years.

Bottom: *Alvin*'s manipulator arm picks up a large clam from the Galápagos Rift in 1977. Scientists can also use the mechanical arm to maneuver a net through the water to collect clumps of animals.

Almost a year earlier, the Woods Hole scientist Fred Grassle had used *Alvin*'s mechanical arms to mark with a file the growing edges of a bunch of mussels. The notches would provide a reference point for Rich and Howard Sanders. But first they had to locate the mussel bed. It took them several hours just to find the small white cubes that acted as signposts to mark the experiment. Rich was amazed. "It's a huge ocean, and you go down and mark one mussel with a file and put it back down, and you can get that needle out of a haystack again."

Once they had located the mussels, Rich and Howard had to collect some. *Alvin*'s pilot used the jawlike pincer at the end of one of *Alvin*'s mechanical arms to draw a large net sideways through the clump of mussels. He placed the samples in a large bucket on the rectangular platform below *Alvin*'s nose, just in front of the viewing port.

The insulated collecting bucket keeps the animals at the temperature they came from, only a few degrees above freezing. When the scientists get everything back on board the mother ship, they transfer the samples into refrigerated aquariums. If they want to keep an animal alive they would need to repressurize it in a special separate container.

The research crew sorted all the animals they brought back to the surface. They took samples of soft tissues for genetic and microscopic studies and then prepared the mussel shells for growth-rate analysis back at Woods Hole and their university laboratories.

Rich remembers the wonder he felt the night he returned from the abyss, sitting on the deck of the support ship, talking with another scientist until four o'clock in the morning. "Everything I wanted in terms of marine biology, I felt I had accomplished during that dive. If I never made it back, I would have achieved my goal, my whole purpose for getting into the field."

When Rich studied the mussels he and Howard Sanders retrieved, he discovered that vent animals grew remarkably fast during the short period from when they were marked with the file. Compared to the typical deep-sea clam that had grown a third of an inch in a hundred years, one species of hydrothermal vent clam (*Calyptogena magnifica*) grew three hundred times as fast.

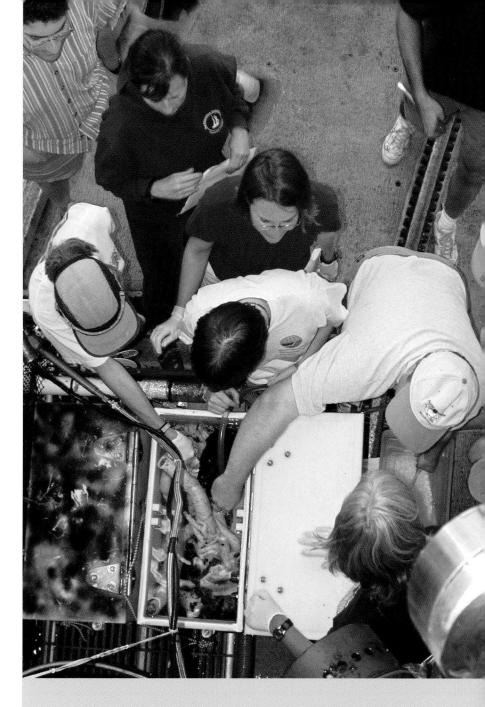

Scientists examine the contents of the bio box brought back to the surface from a hydrothermal vent. The chalky gray tubes of *Riftia* tubeworms are prominent among the other animals.

Alvin sits on the bottom of the ocean, its mechanical arm deployed in front of the pilot's window, a spotlight illuminating the deep.
The science platform with its collecting gear and sample baskets lies underneath the light.

Mollusks on a Fast Track to Survival

When Rich was growing up, he was one of those kids who loved to play in the local creek, chasing frogs and salamanders. The Boy Scouts gave him the chance to get out in nature, and he took it for all its worth, first becoming an Eagle Scout, then getting elected to scouting's national honor society called the Order of the Arrow. When it came time for Rich to go to college, studying biology made the most sense, based on everything he enjoyed doing. "You start out doing what you're doing because it's the romance and passion that attracts you," recalls Rich. "The little kid in you hasn't grown up and wants to play . . . to find out some of the fundamental secrets of the universe. Then I realized I could do these kinds of things in the real world and even get paid for it!"

After Rich Lutz's first amazing dive to a hydrothermal vent, he decided to focus his study on the deep sea. After he got his doctorate from the University of Maine and did more post-graduate study at Yale University from 1977 to 1979, Rich spent more than a decade traveling to just about every known site of hydrothermal vent activity around the world. He and his fellow scientists were pioneers, discovering new vents and new vent communities every year.

Rich Lutz climbs down the narrow entryway of the conning tower that leads to the six and a half feet in diameter sphere, which he will share with a pilot and another observer.

Top: Mussels retrieved from the Galápagos mussel bed site in 1979 show where researchers made a mark with a file and the growth that took place afterward.

Bottom: Rich embedded pieces of clamshells in a bed of epoxy glue and used *Alvin* to leave them at various distances from hydrothermal vents. When he returned to the experiment later he collected the shell fragments and measured how much shell had dissolved. By understanding how much time it takes for a measured amount of clamshell to dissolve, Rich could predict how much new shell might develop in a living clam, and then how fast it might grow.

Everywhere Rich went, he conducted experiments to try to answer the questions that fascinated him. How do mussels, clams, and other mollusks survive in this forbidding environment? How fast do they grow and why? How do they compare with their shallow-water cousins? And how do new communities develop when one vent stops producing hydrogen sulfide and a new one suddenly appears tens if not hundreds of miles away?

To learn how fast clams and mussels grew near hydrothermal vents and how old they were, Rich continued to record shell growth with the "mark-recapture" technique. Rich also analyzed how clamshells dissolved over time. Measuring clamshell dissolution helps when Rich finds dead clams at an inactive hydrothermal vent. "We can estimate how long it has been since the hydrothermal vent was active," Rich explains. "We can do this by assuming that all of the clams died when the hot water at the vents 'shut off' and then measuring how much of the clamshell has dissolved since it was alive. If we know how long it takes for that much shell to have dissolved, we can then make a good estimate of how long it has been since the vent was active."

Rich and his colleagues at Yale also tested for radioactive chemicals in the shells of the clams. Because scientists know how fast radium and uranium decay, they can determine the age of the mollusks by measuring the chemicals left in the shells.

Vent mollusks can grow as large as a dinner plate—up to twelve inches. How? Mussels and clams are filter feeders. Like little vacuum cleaners, they suck in the water around them, trapping and absorbing organic matter they use for food and then throwing out the leftover waste. There is much less organic matter in the deep ocean than there is in the Chesapeake Bay, where Rich had conducted experiments. But around hydrothermal vents, deep-sea mollusks usually find enough of this food to survive, at least for a while. Filter feeding is not the most important means of survival for deep-sea clams and mussels, however. Certain kinds of bacteria form partnerships with host animals living inside these mollusks' gills. The bacteria, in turn, nourish the clams and mussels with the sugars and carbohydrates they manufacture from hydrogen sulfide.

Until the discovery of hydrothermal vents, most evidence indicated that life in the deep ocean developed very slowly. Rich and his colleagues were able to come to a different conclusion. The hydrothermal vents are unstable places where change comes quickly and unexpectedly. Because the vents provide a source of abundant energy found nowhere else in the deep ocean, the animals that live here grow much faster than other deep-sea animals. They grow so quickly that they compare to animals on the very surface of the ocean, where sunlight is the source of development.

Clamshells are placed on the bottom to determine how fast the shells dissolve. Experiments like this help scientists figure out how long it has been since hydrothermal vents were active, and how fast clams grow.

Black smokers like this one create chimney-like spires that pour hot liquid from under the earth's crust.

Explorer of the Deep

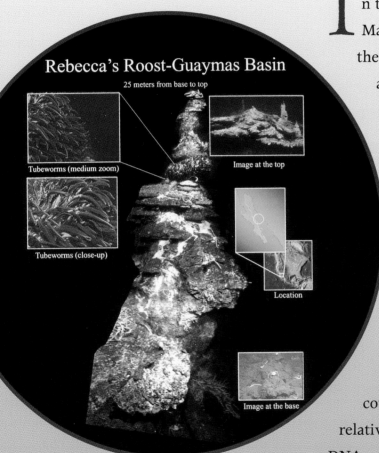

Rebecca's Roost-Guaymas Basin

25 meters from base to top

Tubeworms (medium zoom)

Tubeworms (close-up)

Image at the top

Location

Image at the base

Fifty-three separate images were pieced together here in a collage to represent a hydrothermal structure called Rebecca's Roost in the southern trough of the Guaymas Basin. Rich Lutz named it after his daughter Rebecca.

I n the early 1990s, Rich joined several expeditions nicknamed the Magical Mystery Tour. With other scientists, he toured around the world, exploring hydrothermal vent communities to try to answer several important questions. Where did the species of mussels and clams found at hydrothermal vents come from? Were they closely related to species found in tide pools or on rocky shores? And were species of clams found at one hydrothermal vent in the Atlantic Ocean related to species found far away in the Pacific? Rich worked with a geneticist, Bob Vrijenhoek, to answer these questions. Collecting samples of the genetic material from clams and mussels became an important part of each dive to the ocean floor.

The evidence they collected suggests that the deep-ocean mollusks are only distantly related to their shallow-water counterparts. Deep-ocean mollusks probably diverged from their relatives 30 to 50 million years ago. However, a comparison of the DNA—the molecules in the nucleus of cells that contain their genetic

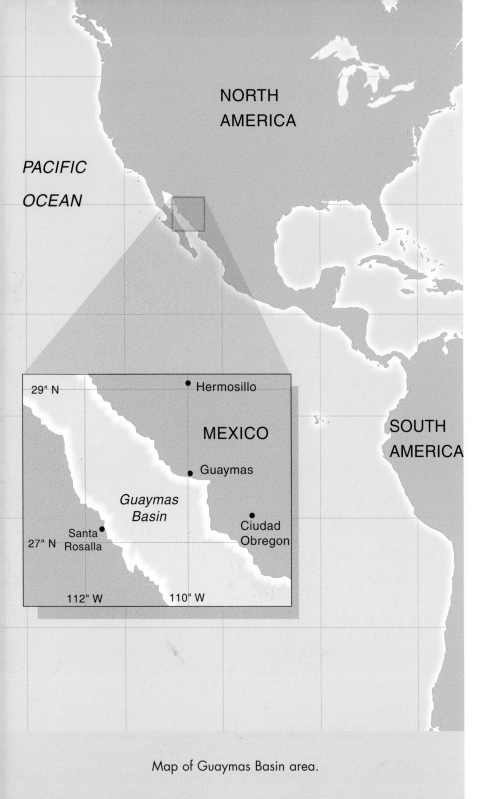

NORTH
AMERICA

PACIFIC

OCEAN

SOUTH
AMERICA

29" N   • Hermosillo

MEXICO

• Guaymas

*Guaymas
Basin*

Santa •
27" N Rosalla

• Ciudad
Obregon

112" W   110" W

Map of Guaymas Basin area.

code—of mussels at one hydrothermal vent with the DNA of mussels at another vent hundreds of miles away found them remarkably similar. Rich believes that larvae travel over long distances in deep-sea currents.

The Magical Mystery Tour took Rich to the Guaymas Basin in the Pacific Ocean's Sea of Cortez, where he discovered three giant chimneys called black smokers. Black smokers are one of the deep sea's most spectacular kinds of hydrothermal vents. Made of sulfur-bearing minerals called sulfides, they produce clouds of dark, hot fluid with temperatures up to 750 degrees Fahrenheit. The black color comes from minerals dissolved in the fluid. When this superheated water meets the cold of the surrounding ocean water, minerals precipitate out of the water, creating chimneys that look like giant smokestacks.

As watch leader aboard the ship from eight in the morning until noon and from eight in the evening until midnight, Rich recorded new discoveries and monitored all the ship's activities to make sure nothing went wrong. As is the tradition for watch leaders, Rich got to name the three black smokers he found on his watch in the Guaymas Basin. He called them Rebecca's, Ryan's, and Richie's Roosts after his children. Each of the chimneys was the height of a five-story building. Some chimneys can grow as tall as a fifteen-story building!

Years later Rich discovered another hydrothermal vent as part of the Magical Mystery Tour in the South Pacific. He described it as one of the most beautiful vents and named it Sarah's Spring after his wife.

ALVIN

Constructed in 1964 and named after the Woods Hole oceanographer Allyn Vine, who helped develop a national program for manned undersea vehicles, *Alvin* was the world's first deep-sea research submersible. While other deep-sea submersibles now exist, *Alvin* has remained vital to the United States deep-sea oceanographic community.

Known by some as "Water Baby" or "the ball," *Alvin* can't stay submerged for as long as some other deep-sea submarines—its normal dive time is between six and ten hours. The two Russian-made Mirs have more battery power and can remain under water for over twice as long. *Alvin* can't go as deep as some other submersibles. The Japanese Shinkai 6500 goes to depths of 19,500 feet (3.7 miles), whereas *Alvin*'s maximum recommended depth is 14,764 feet (about 2.8 miles).

Despite these apparent shortcomings, *Alvin* is one of deep-sea science's most remarkable tools. Rich Lutz calls it "the workhorse of the deep for more than thirty years." "Of all the submersibles that exist," says Rich, "it is the one that has logged by far the greatest amount of science time. It is a fine-tuned machine, often held together seemingly by rubber bands, tie wraps, and ring and hose clamps, yet it is a machine that is highly adaptable to anything you would want to do."

Scientists climb into *Alvin* through the conning tower, a raised structure on the submarine's deck. The pressure-resistant titanium sphere keeps them safe. Titanium weighs very little but has the incredible strength and resiliency to withstand pressure as high as 6,415 pounds per square inch.

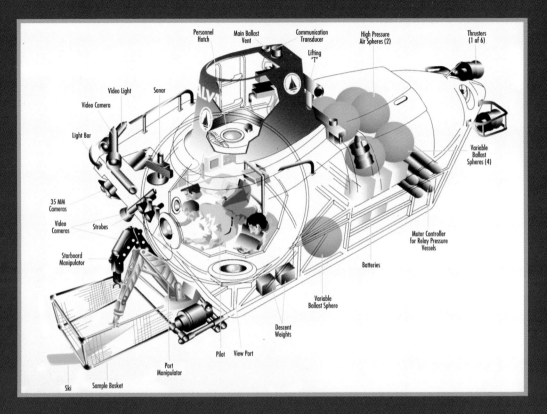

This schematic shows *Alvin*'s exterior and interior as of 2001. Since its maiden voyage in 1964, *Alvin* has been retooled and updated periodically to take advantage of new technologies.

After it has traveled along railroad-like tracks on the deck of the *RV Atlantis,* leaving its protective hangar behind, *Alvin* gets hoisted into the air and carefully deposited on the surface of the ocean. A support diver stands ready to release the tow-line once *Alvin* is floating.

The navigational gear, video monitors, sonar readouts, gyro compass, carbon dioxide scrubbers (to keep the air safe to breathe), and emergency rebreathers share the 6.5-foot diameter space with the pilot and two scientists. Add special camera equipment and the living quarters turn into a giant sandwich of arms, legs, and machines. There are only three small viewing ports in the submersible's rugged sphere: one in the front of the sub for the pilot and two others, port and starboard, where scientists sit to take notes and photographs. The viewing ports are made of acrylic plastic three and a half inches thick and only five inches in diameter on the inside of the sub.

A trip to the bottom of the ocean may begin in sparkling sunlight and blue sky. Launched by a giant crane at the back of a mother ship such as *RV Atlantis,* the sub sinks slowly, spinning in a circle. Six hundred pounds of steel bars packed along *Alvin*'s flanks draw it downward. No one inside notices the spinning, only the slow disappearance of sunlight and the increasingly colder temperatures. Water condenses on the inner skin of the titanium sphere, and the titanium becomes cold to the touch. At about 3,280 feet, *Alvin* passes the average depth of the ocean's deepest-diving mammal, the sperm whale. It takes about an hour to reach a mile below the surface, a dark and mysterious underwater universe.

IMAX photographer Bill Reeve checks a video monitor as he tracks a fish swimming near *Alvin.*

The *RV Atlantis* lowers *Alvin* into the water for a dive, monitored by divers in a support boat.

Researchers aboard *Alvin* use instruments like the one shown here to sample the fluids coming from hydrothermal vents.

Inside a Volcanic Eruption

In April 1991 Rich Lutz was a mile and a half deep in the Pacific Ocean at a hydrothermal vent site called Nine North, five hundred miles southwest of Acapulco, Mexico. When *Alvin*'s spotlights came on, they illuminated a scene of death and destruction. What had been a rich oasis of life was now a graveyard of glassy black rocks. An ashy-colored storm of deep-ocean bacteria flew all around.

The name Nine North comes from the site's latitude coordinates on a map. Latitude is the distance in degrees north or south of the equator. Longitude measures degrees east and west of the prime meridian. Nine North is nine degrees north of the equator, longitude 104 degrees west, at the intersection of the Cocos and Pacific plates on the crest of the East Pacific Rise. In an area of the rift valley that had once contained fourteen thriving communities of animals and many black smokers, the scientists on the expedition soon realized that they were in the middle of a volcanic eruption that was killing everything in sight.

Sometime between March 26 and April 6, 1991, a section of the East Pacific Rise erupted in the Pacific Ocean. Scientists found tumbled-down structures and volcanic glass called obsidian, the result of lava cooling rapidly when it encounters the cold water of the deep.

These mollusks called limpets, which were collected at Nine North in April 1991, have been "steamed on the half shell" after the volcanic eruption that occurred in the area.

The glossy black glass Rich saw everywhere is called obsidian, formed when lava cools suddenly. In one area they later named Tubeworm Barbecue, the scientists found a graveyard of charred, cooked tubeworms, clams, mussels, and other invertebrates littering the sea floor.

"In 1991," Rich recalls, "each of us had the opportunity to go down and witness firsthand this volcanic eruption. What we had was essentially a snowstorm of bacteria that we were flying through. The pilot would not descend into this cloudy cauldron for fear of finding hot molten lava inside."

The bacteria pouring from "snowblower vents" was a sign of rebirth for the community. It showed the scientists that new vents were once again releasing hydrogen sulfide, the life-sustaining source of energy at a hydrothermal vent. "What we are learning," Rich observed, "is that when you have a volcanic eruption you get tremendous quantities of hot water coming out, which have absolutely phenomenal concentrations of hydrogen sulfide." Temperature probes measured a remarkable 752 degrees Fahrenheit in some of the black smoker vents, more than enough heat to melt lead, let alone *Alvin*'s acrylic portholes, the destruction of which would crush the submersible and everyone inside.

Scientists observed bacteria and their associated products spewing from newly opened cracks in the ocean floor called "snowblowers" and blowing 160 feet high.

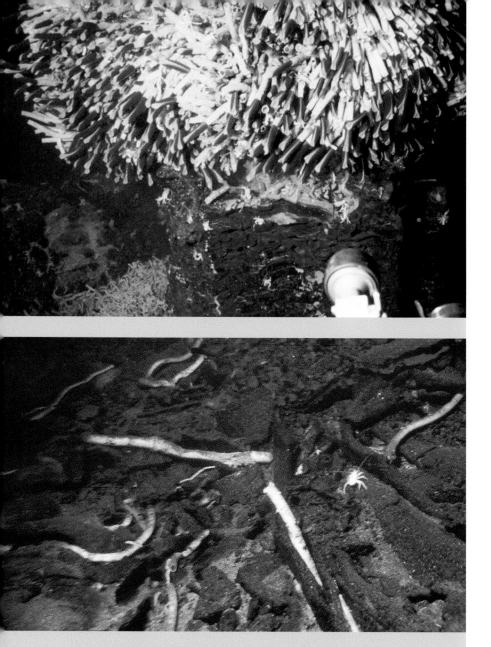

Top: Nicknamed Tubeworm Pillar just after the volcanic eruption in 1991, a group of *Riftia* tubeworms (*at top of photo*) survived because they stood high off the sea floor, away from the flow of hot lava.

Bottom: In April 1991, Nine North was a field of gray ash, fresh lava, and dead tubeworms.

Using a radiometric dating technique similar to the one Rich used to understand the growth of clams and mussels, the scientists gathered samples of the obsidian using *Alvin*'s collecting arms. They knew that a radioactive element in the now-cooled rock called polonium 210 decays at a fixed rate. Using that measurement in growth they later estimated that the eruption date fell within the exact time frame during which Rich and his fellow scientists were exploring the area in *Alvin*. As Rich recalls, "We were effectively in the middle of an ongoing volcanic eruption." He had happened upon something most scientists only dream of—the chance to study the rebirth of a special community of animals from ground zero.

Yellow Brick Road

Once an expert on clams and mussels, Rich found his world expanding. Now a full professor in the Department of Marine and Coastal Sciences at Rutgers University, Rich became project coordinator for a series of returning expeditions to Nine North. Together with teams of geologists, chemists, and other biologists, he and his colleagues would make annual visits to the same oasis in the Pacific. These researchers set out to chronicle the stages of new life as it developed in the deep ocean.

Beginning in March 1992, Rich and his fifty colleagues established an on-the-bottom observatory inside a mile-long section of the ocean floor by placing 210 numbered and coded markers at three- to fifty-foot intervals. Although they paved the ocean bottom with white markers to help them monitor specific animals, they called it the Yellow Brick Road. Like the yellow brick road in *The Wizard of Oz*, it became a symbol of a journey of discovery.

Rich Lutz displays the biomarkers that were created as signposts in the Nine North area. The signs were made of polyethylene to resist corrosion and attached to weights to keep them on the bottom. Because the number may get overgrown as the ocean floor community grows, or the ink may become smudged and unreadable, there are specially coded holes in the marker as well.

NAVIGATION

Deep-submergence vehicles such as *Alvin* and research vessels such as *RV Atlantis* employ a variety of navigational tools to locate objects as small as a clam bed a mile or more deep in the ocean. Before the volcanic eruption at the Nine North site, scientists had already created a detailed image of the sea bottom using a towed "sled" called *Argo*. Using video and still cameras and acoustic (sound) equipment, *Argo* revealed a long, shallow trough at the top of the East Pacific Rise. From this trough periodic volcanic eruptions were paving new ocean floor and pushing the two plates—the Pacific and the Cocos plates—apart.

Research vessels such as the *RV Atlantis* will tow sleds like *Argo II* (shown) for several days at a time. It can be operated around the clock and as deep as 20,000 feet, sending acoustic and video signals via fiberoptic cable to a shipboard control center, where five technicians fly the vehicle, record data, and monitor equipment.

By following this "road" every time they visited the area, the scientists hoped to show how hydrothermal communities changed over time. To ensure that it would remain undisturbed, they made an agreement with other scientists to treat the Nine North study site as a deep-sea sanctuary. Only photography, water temperature probes, and water sampling were allowed. Instead of collecting biological specimens, the scientists would photograph and film the changes as one community of animals died and a new one grew to take its place.

The scientists returned to the same markers year after year for ten years to sample water chemistry for changes in hydrogen sulfide. *Alvin*'s mechanical hands held a heat-resistant temperature probe and a water sampler and maneuvered them directly into the smoker chimneys. The measuring instruments looked like giant probing fingers.

The researchers programmed cameras that could be left behind in the deep-sea observatory. *Alvin* carried the cameras in a big fiberglass box mounted on its front-end science platform. Scientists positioned the cameras on the research site and set automatic timers. The still camera took a picture with an electronic flash every twelve hours for ten months. The video camera took twenty seconds of video once a day for the same ten-month period. Rich was thrilled by the opportunity to actually "see" the events and growth that occurred each day.

A satellite navigation system called the Global Positioning System (GPS) allows scientists to return to Nine North time after time without getting lost. GPS consists of a system of twenty-four satellites orbiting above the earth that send radio-wave signals to receivers on earth, including receivers on research vessels such as *RV Atlantis*. With these radio signals and synchronized clocks, researchers can pinpoint an exact location on earth.

The GPS system helps the *Alvin* pilot and the observers aboard the *RV Atlantis* determine where they are in the ocean and where they are in relation to each other. Once the *RV Atlantis* has arrived at the coordinates of latitude 9 degrees and 50.1 minutes north, and longitude 104 degrees and 17.5 minutes west, it drops two or three sound-transmitting transponders capable of transmitting and receiving sound signals to and from each other, *Alvin,* and the research vessel above. Computers on board the vehicles interpret signals from all sources to give an accurate location of *Alvin* on the ocean floor to within thirty feet.

Above: One of *Alvin*'s pilots, Bruce Strickrott, sits in the mother ship *RV Atlantis,* monitoring communications with another pilot who is aboard *Alvin* a mile or more below. He can both talk with the pilot and plot *Alvin*'s direction and distance traveled on a video monitor to his right.

Left: This artist's recreation of a section of the Nine North region where the volcanic eruption took place in 1991 shows the results after the lava lake subsided. Hydrothermal vents are most often found along such valleys' margins. *Alvin*, shown at top, would be almost invisible if drawn to scale.

This scene shows the edge of the hydrothermal vent community where squat lobsters and small worms called serpulids live, visible as squiggly lines on the bottom.

The Rise of Life in the Deep Sea

Jericho worms, a kind of tubeworm whose scientific name is *Tevnia jericho-nana,* are the first tubeworms to colonize a hydrothermal vent community as it grows from ground zero. *Tevnia* tubes have a characteristic accordion look and are slenderer than the other tubeworm species, *Riftia.*

When *Alvin* observers returned to Nine North in 1992, the snowstorm of bacteria had tapered off to scattered flurries. Larger animals were appearing—an assortment of scavengers and grazers such as worms. The first colonizers of ground zero were consuming the bacterial snow as fast as it was being produced. In particular, areas around the smokers contained hordes of crabs called brachyurans (BRACH-ee-yer-ans). These short-tailed true crabs feed on mats of bacteria and other microbes, as well as pieces of dead tubeworms or other animals. Rich remembers seeing larvae of these crabs swarming like hundreds of thousands of sand fleas in "crab nurseries" right after the 1991 eruption. They were now adults about the size of New England rock crabs and had hearty appetites.

Small invertebrates called copepods (COPE-ah-pods) and amphipods (AM-fih-pods) were thriving. The copepods used their little swimmerets, appendages like tiny arms or wings,

to keep them afloat and to help them graze on bacteria. Amphipods, often no bigger than fleas, appeared in clouds around warmer water coming out of the vents.

Eel-like animals called zoarcids (zo-ARE-sids) were among the first fish on the scene. Also known as eelpouts because their mouth shape makes them look as if they are pouting, they consume everything from bacteria in mats to shrimp and other small invertebrates. Pockets of the white or rust-colored (due to iron staining) Jericho tubeworms (also called *Tevnia* after their scientific name) were the first tubeworms. Although mature tubeworms live stationary lives attached to a surface like a rock, their larvae can travel significant distances. About a foot long and as wide as a pencil, Jericho worms live inside a tube made in part out of the same material as the shell of a crab. They survive by absorbing the hydrogen sulfide fluids of a nearby vent. Hundreds of them surround a vent, grouped in a pattern that looks like a bull's-eye.

Jericho worms live cooperatively with bacteria similar to the way clams and mussels do, acting as hosts for the bacteria and getting sugars and carbohydrates in return. These tubeworms do not have a stomach or a mouth and cannot feed on their own. They are entirely dependent on "food" obtained from the bacteria. This sharing, or symbiotic, relationship between worm and bacteria allows both to benefit and to grow much faster than other animals in the deep.

Evolution of a Full-Blown Community

R ich returned to Nine North in December 1993 with a team of biologists, geologists, geochemists, documentary filmmakers, and photographers from *National Geographic*. As he waited in the control room of *RV Atlantis,* Rich listened in as the first group of scientists went down to see what changes had taken place over the previous year. "Anything could have happened," he remembers. "We could have reset a clock with another volcanic eruption, we could have had the communities die, it could have been one of the most disastrous stage sets imaginable."

But as the crew stood by, a voice from the deep came over the intercom with the announcement, "It's packed." To Rich, those words said it all. "From *Riftia* [another kind of tubeworm] and *Tevnia* to crabs, amphipods, and zoarcid fish, it was a full-blown rose garden of activity. An oasis of life on the bottom of the ocean sprang up in a period of time that no one in the biological community could have predicted or believed. Truth was stranger than fantasy."

Researchers have found that vent tubeworms are the fastest growing marine invertebrate on the planet. These clusters of the *Riftia pachyptila* and *Tevnia jerichonana* are examples of this productiveness.

35

This close-up of the *Riftia* tubeworms' red plumes reveals one of the secrets to their survival. The red color is due to hemoglobin. The worm uses it to transport life-giving hydrogen sulfide from the surrounding vents to bacteria living inside the worm.

The Jericho worm community was much more extensive now, forming bulls-eye patches with hundreds of animals per patch. But the tubeworm that now captured Rich's attention was called *Riftia* after its scientific name, *Riftia pachyptila*. It had always been one of the stars of Nine North hydrothermal vent communities before the eruption. To scientists, it signals a maturing community.

When taking in the hydrogen sulfide, oxygen, and carbon dioxide from the surrounding water, *Riftia* extends a plume of blood red tentacles woven into a tight mass that looks like a curled tongue. The feathery plume's red color comes from a chemical called hemoglobin (HEEM-oh-globe-in), which seizes and transports the life-giving hydrogen sulfide to the worm's specialized tissue called the trophosome (TROPH-oh-soam). Since *Riftia* has no mouth or stomach, it relies on the bacteria living inside its trophosome for food.

In addition to the huge populations of amphipods and copepods seen in previous years, the Yellow Brick Road now contained a host of new creatures, including alvinellid (alvin-EL-id) worms, strange jellyfish called siphonophores (si-FON-oh-fors), mollusks called limpets, and galatheid (gal-ah-THEE-id) crabs.

Alvinellid worms such as this creature with red tentacles can survive in some of the hottest environments in the ocean.

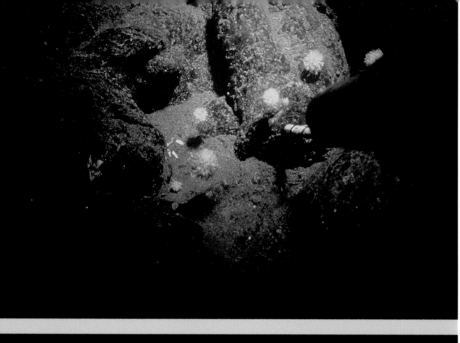

The clumps of dandelion flower–shaped creatures are called siphonophores. About the size of a ping-pong ball, they consist of colonies of individual animals, each with special functions.

Researchers named the alvinellid worms in honor of the submarine *Alvin*. Among the ocean's most heat-tolerant creatures, they often live on the sides of black smokers. Alvinellids have been seen swimming in and out of waters over 212 degrees Fahrenheit (the boiling point of water at sea level). Their red plumes emerge from a tube six or more feet long to capture food in the surrounding currents.

Siphonophores are closely related to the Portuguese man-of-war, the purple and pink jelly animal that floats like a transparent bag at the surface of tropical waters with its tentacles hanging below it. Siphonophore bodies are composed of groups of specialized cells. Each colony of cells has a different function. Some specialize in reproduction, others in digestion, and they all share the same gelatinous home.

A limpet looks like a stone hat with a ridge at the top. It uses a filelike tongue on its fleshy underside to graze on bacteria in the deep sea, whereas its cousins in tide pools scrape algae in shallow, sunlit waters. Galatheid crabs, called squat lobsters because they look like short, thick-waisted lobsters, are like vultures. Often solitary, these crabs scavenge dead and dying animals for food.

But where were the mussels and clams that Rich Lutz had spent his life studying? In December 1993, they were still nowhere to be seen at Nine North.

Four months later, in March 1994, an expedition to study fluids coming out of vents at Nine North collected more evidence for what scientists already knew. Rich was not on this expedition, but he followed its results closely. When *Alvin* returned to a vent chimney that had been knocked over in December 1993, researchers found that a new spire more than twenty feet tall had grown in its place.

The giant six-foot *Riftia* tubeworms had grown an average of a tenth of an inch (two to three millimeters) a day. "Now we have unambiguous evidence," Rich observed, "that not only are things growing fast, but in the case of tubeworms, they are growing faster than any other marine invertebrate on the planet. Things are growing at a phenomenally rapid rate in a deep-sea system that is very different from a normal deep-sea system."

A colony of giant tubeworms called *Riftia pachyptila* photographed using an IMAX camera at the Nine North site. Porcelain-white vent crabs are seen throughout the colony along with a number of pink fish known as eelpouts.

Photos of the shells of this giant white clam, *Calyptogena magnifica,* shown here in the Pacific Ocean area known as Clam Acres, were important clues that life in the deep sea was more varied and complex than anyone had imagined.

The Year of the Mussels

Captured on camera and in video footage, the Nine North community continued to change. In 1995, some new chimneys suddenly appeared in certain regions. In other areas, previously existing black smokers had changed into even higher and more complex chimneys. In still other vent regions, however, the hydrogen sulfide flow began to weaken and change. By now, some of the new vent colonies were already dead. Without the ingredients for chemosynthesis, the bacteria died and so did all the organisms dependent on them.

Five years after the eruption, mussels had begun to surround most of the tubeworm colonies in the Nine North area. Rich had predicted this from his work in other deep-sea vents around the world. Clams and mussels don't thrive in high concentrations of the poisonous hydrogen sulfide. They appear only when the flow is reduced.

Fifty-five months after the eruption, every tubeworm community but one was surrounded by the mussel *Bathymodiolus thermophilus*, which was able to encroach once hydrogen sulfide levels in the vent water decreased. The mussels eventually replace tubeworms as the dominant presence in vent communities. Mussels are symbiotic with deep-sea bacteria, but unlike tubeworms they are not entirely dependent on the bacteria.

Where do the mollusks come from? It is thought that they are the offspring of clams and mussels living in cracks and crevices tens or even hundreds of miles away. These mollusks eject sperm and eggs into the surrounding water, where fertilization takes place, eventually producing swimming larvae about 0.3 millimeters long. Deep-ocean currents carry the larvae, sometimes transporting them many miles. The larvae eventually respond to cues, such as increased temperature, high concentrations of hydrogen sulfide, or the presence of bacteria. All these cues indicate hydrothermal vent environments.

The appearance of clams and mussels signals the approach of the final phase in the life of a hydrothermal vent. Sometimes these mollusks even cause the community's collapse. Mussel larvae will settle in cracks and crevices and begin to grow. As the mussels increase in size and the hydrogen sulfide concentration decreases in the area, the mussels migrate (using their specialized "feet") and attach themselves to the tubeworms causing them to sag, pulling them away from the precious life-giving hydrogen sulfide coming out of nearby vents. In addition, the mussels themselves consume most of the hydrogen sulfide that may be present. Deprived of nourishment, the *Riftia* will die, leaving behind a community dominated by mussels and clams.

Even the clams and mussels eventually disappear as the vent flow continues to diminish. Clams die first because they depend more on the bacteria living in their gills. Without bacteria, mussels can survive for a while by filtering food from the surrounding water, but unless new vents renew the hydrogen sulfide, the mussels too will soon die.

From 1991 to 1999, Rich and his colleagues charted a remarkable life cycle at hydrothermal vents, a pattern that parallels the succession of life from a barren landscape to a forest environment. Deep-sea succession begins with total destruction by a volcanic eruption, just as a forest fire renews life on land. New cracks and vents then emerge in the ocean floor, bringing a fresh source of energy and food. First comes a snowstorm of bacteria. It becomes dinner for tiny shrimplike animals such as copepods and amphipods and scavengers such as vent crabs and eelpouts. Jericho worms are the first of the tubeworm species to arrive, followed by the giant *Riftia* tubeworm. Now snail-like limpets, squat lobsters, feather duster worms, and octopi have joined the banquet. By the fifth year, *Riftia* anchor a thriving community—the equivalent of a maturing forest on land. Then clams and mussels mark the final phase before the community needs a new eruption to begin over again.

These images summarize the changes that took place at the Nine North study area beginning with the volcanic eruption in 1991 and continuing to 1999. All of the photos show the kinds of animals that took up residence around biomarker 119. Shortly after the eruption, mats of bacteria and other microbes began to form near the vents and pieces were forced up in the water column by fluids from the vent (A and B). The tubeworm *Tevnia jerichonana* appeared within a year of the eruption but was gradually replaced by the larger *Riftia pachyptila* (C and D). The mature *Riftia* community (E) supported perhaps the biggest mass of biological organisms of any stage in this cycle. But by eight years after the eruption, the mussel *Bathymodiolus thermophilus* invaded this community and eventually replaced the *Riftia* (F). By this time, marker 119 was completely buried and the seascape had changed dramatically.

Rich explains the excitement of witnessing the mysteries of the deep. "It's as if you worked your entire career trying to answer the question of how fast the animals grow at hydrothermal vents, and you had a lot of assumptions . . . but your best guess is that they grow pretty fast. And then, you look at two photographs of Nine North side by side. One shows the site in 1992 with no *Riftia* at all. The other shows the same area in 1993 with five-foot-high tubeworms. And you say, 'Any questions?'"

The same cycle has probably sustained this oasis in the deep sea since its beginnings. The hot magma of volcanoes destroys one community, but new ones appear at different sites along the mid-ocean ridge. With the death of a community, the seeds of rebirth wait for a chemical cue or change in temperature. New life will appear along the Nine North ridge, sometimes a year later, sometimes ten or a hundred years later. But life will return.

Top: Ghostly lava formations left behind after the volcanic eruption in April 1991 give the appearance of the ruins of an underwater city.

Bottom: A pink eelpout and several vent crabs meander among a field of tubeworms at the Nine North site.

New Eyes on the Deep Ocean

In November 1999, Rich brought a new group of observers to Nine North. Through his work as Director of the Center for Deep-Sea Ecology and Biotechnology at Rutgers University, Rich escorted the IMAX film producer Stephen Low, a film crew, and the *National Geographic* photographer Emory Kristof to the East Pacific Rise. If Stephen could get the images he needed, he would bring "new eyes" to the utter darkness of the deep ocean in an IMAX film called *Volcanoes of the Deep Sea*. The film, Rich hoped, would share the wonders of this strange new world with an audience far beyond the scientific community.

For Rich and Stephen, these new eyes were a revolutionary camera system. Like the invention of the microscope or telescope, this breakthrough in technology would help scientists answer questions they had not been able to explore before. "A few years ago we put up a remarkable thing in space called the Hubble telescope," Rich said. "It enabled us to look into the depths of outer space like we have

As chief scientist on a cruise to several different hydrothermal vent areas, Rich Lutz reviews and approves preparations for the day's dive. IMAX film director Stephen Low stands next to him.

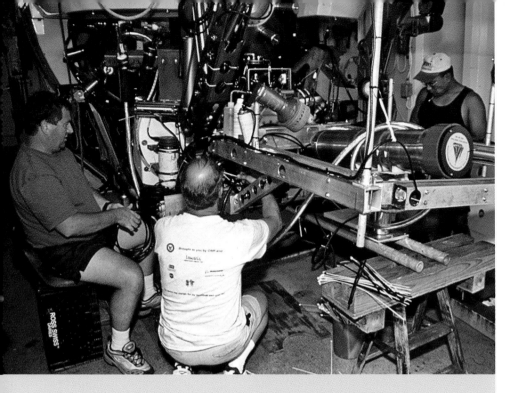

On this expedition to the Mid-Atlantic Ridge in 2001, the IMAX director Stephen Low and his crew packed the front of *Alvin* with extra lights and this high-definition camera with a yellow lens cap. This particular camera allowed the filmmakers to get very detailed close-ups of even the smallest animals they encountered.

never been able to look before. The camera systems we have on the sub here enable us to look into the depths of inner space as we have never looked before and uncover some of the real secrets of the universe."

As its name suggests (Image to the MAXimum), IMAX technology makes an audience feel surrounded by the action, a kind of virtual reality almost as powerful as the film itself. Each frame of film that runs through the giant IMAX projector measures more than two inches wide. The image projected on a screen sixty-five feet high and eighty-five feet wide remains exceptionally sharp and clear.

Stephen, a veteran of deep-sea photography from his earlier IMAX film about the discovery of the sunken ocean liner *Titanic,* faced a number of challenges. First he had to load the IMAX camera through *Alvin*'s narrow conning tower, only a foot and a half wide. The sub would protect the camera from the intense water pressure.

Getting the camera into the sub was only the beginning. Because the front porthole was the best place to do the filming, the pilot had to steer by using live images taken by video cameras mounted outside the sub and displayed on a video screen inside the crowded titanium sphere.

The biggest challenge of all was to get enough light to make a film that would be projected onto a screen the size of a six-story apartment building. Stephen and Rich wanted to show the whole community of animals—smokers, tubeworms, walls of lava—and their relationship to one another. And they wanted to do this in the darkest place on the planet. As Stephen remarked at the time, "It's the difference between lighting the Houston Astrodome or lighting a small bathroom."

To provide the necessary 4,400 watts of light, Stephen used every inch available on *Alvin*'s front end to hold pressure-resistant lights. To give the pictures even more depth, one of the two erector-set-like manipulator arms held a

Stephen Low prepares the IMAX camera to shoot out of the pilot's view port.

powerful 1,200-watt "modeling" light. As *Alvin* glided through the inky darkness of the ocean, it looked like a night watchman carrying a lantern in the form of an enormous chandelier. The little sub shone with sixteen times the light an *Alvin* pilot would normally use to maneuver.

Not only was the film spectacular, but the more powerful camera systems created close-up images that furthered Rich's understanding of hydrothermal vents. Rich observed, "You could distinguish individual species of limpets using a macro lens with a high-definition system. It lets you do everything from identify species to see whole new members of the community you couldn't see because you didn't have the resolution prior to that. It was like bringing a microscope down to the bottom of the ocean."

47

The future of deep-sea exploration is full of promise and potential. Exploring the abyss may lead to amazing break-throughs, from the discovery of new chemicals that can improve our health, to a new understanding about how life on earth began. This computer-generated image used in the IMAX film *Volcanoes of the Deep Sea* shows a new area of the Atlantic Ocean called Lost City, discovered in 2001. Lost City is made of limestone like the structure of a coral reef, but it is formed by a different process in the deep ocean.

Unanswered Questions

Many mysteries remain for Rich to solve. Scientists have explored a lot more of outer space than the deep ocean. Although they have mapped nearly 100 percent of the surface of Venus, they've charted only .001 to 1 percent of the ocean floor. Scientists discover new species on nearly every dive, and more than 95 percent of the life forms they find there are new to science.

Rich still doesn't completely understand how different animals migrate from one deep-sea vent to another. He hopes to answer this question by working with other scientists, including DNA specialists. The discoveries at Nine North revolutionized our understanding of how hydrothermal vent communities live, die, and get reborn, but there are many other secrets of the deep sea.

Someday Rich would like to descend to the deepest part of the ocean, the Marianas Trench. An expedition in the 1960s made it there, but it stayed just twenty minutes. As a part of the ocean where chemosynthetic communities should exist, this area undoubtedly holds many new unidentified species.

Rich and his son Ryan sit in *Alvin*'s titanium capsule on a return trip to Nine North in May 2005.

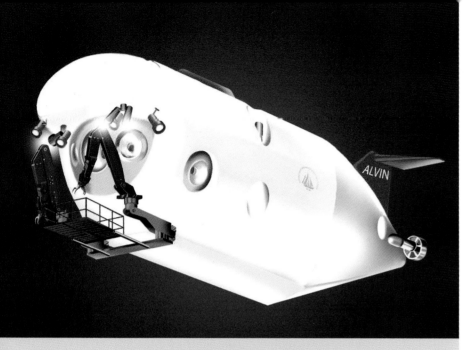

Top: An artist's concept of a new *Alvin* yet to be constructed makes additions that include improved science capabilities, increased depth capability, increased bottom time, improved fields of view, and increased access to the sea floor.

Bottom: An artist's concept of a NASA-launched probe exploring the bottom of an ocean lying beneath a thick layer of ice that covers the surface of Europa.

"One of my dreams would be to go back to the Marianas Trench," says Rich. "It would represent the ultimate because it is the deepest place that we know on the planet."

Perhaps the biggest mystery of all about this strange world of hydrothermal vents still remains unresolved. Did life on earth begin there after the planet was born four and a half billion years ago? Some scientists think tiny microorganisms called Archaea (ar-KAY-ah) may be a key to unlock this mystery. Certain kinds of Archaea thrive in conditions very similar to what existed when the earth was created. Temperatures were extremely hot, and there were lots of volcanic gases and minerals like sulfur, methane, hydrogen, and carbon dioxide, an environment much like hydrothermal vents today.

To further explore this intriguing idea, NASA plans to launch its Europa orbiter to the planet Jupiter in 2008. Two of Jupiter's moons, Io and Europa, show signs of volcanic activity. If an orbiter probe can get beneath Europa's thick layer of ice, scientists think they may find key ingredients for the development of life as we know it at hydrothermal vents. Wouldn't that be amazing? Finding Archaea and life in outer space may someday help us understand how life on earth began. Where else might these strange worlds exist, and what might we learn from them?

For Rich Lutz, each dive to the hidden frontier of the deep holds the chance of uncovering more clues and the challenge of putting the puzzle pieces together.

Several giant *Riftia* tubeworms cling on the side of a chimney at Nine North. The smaller white tubes are those of a small worm known as *Alvinella*, named after the submarine *Alvin*.

Acknowledgments

Diving to a Deep-Sea Volcano has endured an unexpectedly long birth, almost, it seems, as long as the life cycle of the hydrothermal vent described in the text. I would particularly like to thank Amy Flynn, my editor for this book and for my previous Scientists in the Field book, *Swimming with Hammerhead Sharks,* for her steadfast support, insightful critique, and for pulling all of the pieces together after an earlier manuscript guided by my former editor Emily Linsay. Without the former New England Aquarium president Jerry Schubel I would never have had the opportunity to join a month-long IMAX film crew in its search for hydrothermal vents in the North Atlantic Ocean. Without the guidance and infinite patience of Rich Lutz, the scientist chronicled in this story, I would not have had the story to tell. The Stephen Low film company extended me much-appreciated encouragement and cooperation, beginning with Stephen and Alex Low but including help from Pietro Serapiglia and Lilly Antonecchia. Thanks to Emory Kristof, *National Geographic* contract photographer, for photos and storytelling; to Kristen Kusek, fellow science writer and team leader in the creation of a teacher's guide to the IMAX film *Volcanoes of the Deep Sea;* to the scientists Peter Rona, Tim Shank, Dan Fornari, and Drew Reed for help with images; to the crew of the *RV Atlantis,* and to Bruce Strickrott, *Alvin*'s pilot the day it took me more than two miles deep to the area surrounding a hydrothermal vent called the Snake Pit. Thank you Walter Flaherty and Ed Toomey for support through some difficult rebuilding years at the New England Aquarium, and finally thanks to Amanda Lewis and the Doe Coover Agency for helping me make this possible.

An octopus on the ocean floor not far from
hydrothermal vents at Nine North.

Understanding the Deep Sea

Alvin: A deep-sea submersible operated by the Woods Hole Oceanographic Institution in Massachusetts and named after Woods Hole scientist Allyn Vine. *Alvin* made its first dive in 1964.

Alvinellid worm: Named after the deep-sea submersible *Alvin,* this family of worms has been found in waters from 35.6 to over 212 degrees Fahrenheit, which makes it one of the ocean's most heat-tolerant animals.

Amphipods: Small crustaceans, which, in the deep sea, will swarm like insects looking for food. Beach hoppers or sand fleas are a more familiar kind of amphipod. Many are in the .04 to .39 inches (1–10 mm) size range, but some can be much bigger.

Archaea: A kind of microorganism that can live in high temperatures such as those found in hydrothermal vents and that was only discovered in the 1970s. Archaea's genes and biochemistry make them different from bacteria.

Bacteria: A single-celled microorganism that doesn't have a nucleus.

Black smoker: A chimney structure that looks like a smokestack and forms at hydrothermal vents. The fluid it emits resembles smoke because of the dark minerals it contains, especially iron sulfide (pyrite, also known as "fool's gold"). It can reach temperatures as high as 752 degrees Fahrenheit (400 degrees Centigrade).

Chemosynthesis: A process that creates food (carbohydrates) using the energy from compounds like hydrogen sulfide. Bacteria use this food to form the base of a deep-sea food web. Chemosynthesis does not require sunlight the way photosynthesis does, and can thus take place deep in the ocean.

Chlorophyll: The pigment in plants, algae, and phytoplankton that uses the sun's energy to manufacture food (carbohydrates) from water and carbon dioxide.

Continental drift: See plate tectonics.

Copepods: Small shrimplike crustaceans found in fresh and salt water. Most copepods are a few millimeters long (.08 to .12 inches).

Core: The spherical, innermost part of the earth that is largely made of iron. Its radius is about 1,864 miles (3,000 km).

Crust: The outer layer of the earth that is less dense than the rocks in the mantle below. There are two kinds of crust, one for the ocean and the other for the continents.

Crustaceans: A large class of primarily marine invertebrates that have a hard outer shell and jointed appendages. Lobsters, shrimp, barnacles, and crabs are examples.

DNA: Deoxyribonucleic acid; a complex molecule that holds the genetic code for all living things. DNA is an important part of the chromosomes in the nucleus of a cell.

East Pacific Rise: An area of volcanic activity in the mid-ocean ridge system from south of Easter Island to the Gulf of California.

Ecology: The relationship between organisms and their environment.

Filter feeders: Animals that live mostly on the ocean floor and sift or filter the water for food.

Galatheid crabs: Scavenging crabs found around hydrothermal vents, also called squat lobsters because of their thick, short abdomen.

Gyro compass: A navigational instrument that uses a motor driven gyroscope to determine the geographical north instead of the magnetic north.

Hemoglobin: A protein in red blood cells that gives them their color and binds oxygen for transfer to tissues in the body.

Hubble telescope: Built in 1970 and launched in 1990, the Hubble space telescope orbits 375 miles above the earth and provides views of the planets and stars in the universe that ground-based telescopes cannot.

Hydrogen sulfide (H_2S): A chemical compound composed of two atoms of hydrogen and one of sulfur. It produces a colorless gas that smells like rotten eggs and is poisonous to most living things. In the water that comes out of a hydrothermal vent, however, it is the source of energy that bacteria use to build a food web for hundreds of different animals.

Hydrothermal vent (hydro: water; thermal: heat): An opening in the ocean floor through which warm to very hot mineral-laden water flows from the earth's interior. Hydrothermal vents are found in areas of intense volcanic activity such as spreading centers on ocean ridges. When the hot fluid from vents meets cold ocean-bottom water, it can precipitate as chimneys or smokestacks called black smokers.

IMAX film: A very large format film ten times the size of the thirty-five millimeter film seen in regular movie theaters. It can be projected onto domes or rectangular screens up to eight stories high.

Jericho worms: Another name for tubeworms with the scientific name of *Tevnia jerichonana*. Jericho worms have an accordionlike shape and are much smaller than the giant *Riftia* tubeworms.

Larva (plural larvae): The young, immature form of an animal that changes its structure upon becoming an adult. A tadpole, for example, is the larva of a frog.

Latitude: The distance north and south of the equator in degrees.

Lava: Melted or molten rock that has reached to the surface of the earth.

Limpet: A kind of mollusk or snail that clings with a disclike foot to surfaces such as rocks in a tide pool or tubeworms around hydrothermal vents.

Longitude: A measurement of the distance in degrees east and west of the prime meridian, located outside of London, England.

Magma: Melted or molten rock that remains beneath the earth's surface.

Mantle: Zone of rocky material composed of silica, iron, magnesium, and oxygen that lies between the earth's core and crust. It is the largest layer of the earth's interior, about 1,740 miles (2,800 km) thick.

Marianas Trench: The deepest location in all the oceans, located east of the Philippines in the Pacific Ocean. It is almost seven miles (eleven km) deep, deeper than Mount Everest is tall.

Microbe: An organism whose size range is 1/100 to 1/1,000 of a millimeter, usually a single cell. Archaea and bacteria are examples.

Mid-ocean ridge: A huge underwater mountain range that extends more than 40,000 miles (64,374 km) around the earth. It is at the boundary of two tectonic plates that are moving apart and where molten rock rises to form new ocean-bottom crust.

Mollusk: A group of mostly marine invertebrates with soft, unsegmented bodies and often enclosed in a calcium carbonate shell. Examples are clams, mussels, limpets, snails, squid, and octopi.

Nine North: A hydrothermal vent site in the Pacific Ocean named for its latitude coordinates: nine degrees north of the equator.

Obsidian: Volcanic glass, usually black and rich in iron and magnesium.

Photosynthesis: The process by which green plants absorb the energy of the sun to turn carbon dioxide and water into carbohydrates (used as food) and oxygen.

Plankton: Free-floating, often microscopic plants or animals that live in water and that usually depend on water currents to move them around.

Plate tectonics: The theory that the earth's crust is divided into a number of plates that collide and slide past or under one another at their boundaries.

Precipitation: A process where solids separate out from solution, as happens when the hot, mineral-laden water at a hydrothermal vent meets cold ocean water. This precipitation results in the chimneys or smoke-stacks—black smokers are an example.

Prime meridian: An imaginary line from the North to the South Pole running through Greenwich, England. It has been designated zero longitude and is the base from which all longitude lines are measured.

Protozoan: A group of usually microscopic, single-celled organisms whose most familiar representative is the amoeba.

Radiometric dating technique: A method of determining the age of material that contains radionuclides. The shells of mussels and clams contain such radionuclides.

Rift Valley: A fissure or crack in the earth's crust sometimes thousands of miles long caused by volcanic activity and the separation of tectonic plates.

Riftia: The scientific name (genus) of the giant tubeworms, sometimes over six feet long, discovered around hydrothermal vents. They live inside a tube made for protection and survive by getting nutrition provided by the symbiotic bacteria.

Scavenger: An animal that eats dead or decaying remains.

Siphonophores: A jelly animal related to the Portuguese man-of-war that consists of specialized colonies of cells, some for reproduction and others for feeding, for example.

Snowblower vents: Name given to the stage in the development of a hydrothermal vent at which bacteria or substances they produce "blow" out of a vent, creating a scene similar to that made by a snowmaking machine on a ski slope.

Sonar (SOund NAvigation and Ranging): A system of locating objects by sending sound waves out into the ocean and measuring returning echoes. The farther away the object is, the longer it takes for echoes to return.

Submersible: A term that is often used to distinguish research vehicles such as *Alvin* from a conventional submarine. Submersibles are often deep-water research vessels designed for short visits to the ocean floor.

Succession: The change in the kinds of species and composition of a biological community over time in an ecosystem such as a forest or a hydrothermal vent.

Sulfides: Sulfur-bearing minerals.

Symbiosis: An association between organisms where each benefits without harming the other.

Tectonic plates: Rigid sections of the earth's crust that move about in relation to one another; some involve continents, and others involve the ocean.

Tentacles: Long flexible structures, usually on an animal's head or around its mouth, used for grasping or stinging.

Tevnia: The scientific name (genus) of one of the kinds of tubeworms that live around hydrothermal vents. Also known as Jericho worms.

Titanium: A strong, lightweight metallic element used in making the ball, or the living space, in the *Alvin* submersible.

Transponder: An acoustic device that scientists place near the sea floor to assist submersibles in navigating.

Trophosome: A specialized tissue inside a tubeworm that contains symbiotic bacteria, which provide nutrition to the tubeworm.

Water pressure: The weight of water measured in pounds per square inch. Beginning with 14.7 pounds per square inch at sea level, called one atmosphere of pressure, the pressure of one atmosphere doubles for every

thirty-three feet (ten m) of depth. The water pressure at ninety-nine feet, for example, is 58.8 pounds per square inch.

Zoarcids: The scientific name for eelpouts, the predatory fish that are found around hydrothermal vents. Eelpouts can grow to two feet in length.

Styrofoam coffee cups "shrunk" to about one fifth of their normal size after being attached to the outside of *Alvin* during a dive to a hydrothermal vent site in the Atlantic Ocean called Snake Pit (a depth of about two miles).

Suggestions for Further Reading

Books

Gaines, Richard. *The Explorers of the Undersea World*. New York: Chelsea House Publishing, 1994.

Gowell, Elizabeth Tayntor. *Fountains of Life: The Story of Deep Sea Vents*. London: First Books—Ecosystems; Franklin Watts, 1998.

Kovacs, Deborah. *Dive to the Deep Ocean*. Ocean Explorer series. Austin, N.Y.: Raintree Steck-Vaughn, 2000.

Madin, Kate. *Down to a Sunless Sea: The Strange World of Hydrothermal Vents*. Ocean Explorer series. Austin, N.Y.: Raintree Steck-Vaughn, 2000.

Matsen, Brad. *Incredible Submersible* Alvin *Discovers a Strange Deep-Sea World*. Incredible Deep-Sea Adventures series. Berkeley Heights, N.J.: Enslow Publishers, Inc., 2003.

Taylor, Leighton. *Creeps from the Deep: Life in the Deep Sea*. San Francisco: Chronicle Books, 1997.

Videos

Volcanoes of the Deep Sea. Image Entertainment, 2005. Available from Amazon.com.

Voyage into the Abyss. For free video download, visit www.interridge.org ("Downloads"). For DVD, contact the producer: Future Vision, rcooper@tampabay.rr.com, 727-894-3500.

Web sites

Deep-sea submersible *Alvin*
www.whoi.edu/marops/vehicles/alvin (Woods Hole Oceanographic Institution)
oceanexplorer.noaa.gov/technology/subs/alvin/alvin.html (National Oceanic and Atmospheric Administration)
www.ocean.udel.edu/extreme2001/mission/alvin (University of Delaware)

Hydrothermal vent communities
www.botos.com/marine/vents01.html

National Geographic magazine
www.nationalgeographic.com/ngm/0010/feature/

New England Aquarium
www.neaq.org

NOAA vents program
www.pmel.noaa.gov/vents/home.html

Nova Online —"Into the Abyss"
www.pbs.org/wgbh/nova/abyss

Office of Naval Research
www.onr.navy.mil/focus/ocean/vessels/submersibles1.htm

Science News for Kids
www.sciencenewsforkids.org/articles/20041110/refs.asp

Stephen Low Company
www.stephenlow.com

Volcanoes of the Deep Sea IMAX Film Teacher's Guide
www.cosi.org/visit/theaters/movies/extreme/seavolcanoes
Web site to download a PDF file of the teacher's guide to the IMAX film

Volcanoes of the Deep Sea; also includes information about the film and where it is playing and links to a Stephen Low Company/Rutgers University site, www.volcanoesofthedeepsea.com, that describes the IMAX film, including behind-the-scenes information.

Woods Hole Oceanographic Institution—Dive and Discover: Expeditions to the Seafloor
www.divediscover.whoi.edu

Woods Hole Oceanographic Institution
www.whoi.edu

Scientists and crew members gaze at *Alvin* late at night as the pilots equip the submersible with special lights for the next day's dive. They will need these lights for the huge camera required to make the IMAX film *Volcanoes of the Deep Sea*.

Index